FROM VILLAIN TO VICTOR

A STORY OF GOD'S NEVER-ENDING GRACE

WILLIAM DEW

as told to Jill Dew

Copyright © William Dew 2019

All rights reserved. Copyright under Berne Copyright Convention, Universal Copyright Convention, and Pan-American Copyright Convention. No part of this publication may be reproduced, stored in a retrieval system or transmitted in any form, or by any means, electronic, mechanical, photocopying, recording or otherwise, without the prior written permission of the author, who is the copyright owner.

First published 2019

ISBN 9781091146457

Contents

Dedication	5
Foreword	6
1. The Beginning of the Bruises	9
2. The Teenage Years and Hidden Bruises	13
3. My Life of Crime	17
4. The Florida and Texas Years	24
5. The Arizona/California years	32
6. California Years	42
7. After Prison	55
Update on My Children	69
Final Thoughts	71

Dedication

Thank you to my lovely wife (the high school English teacher) for making this book possible. While visiting me twice a day in the hospital in Thailand we used this time to write this book. I told the stories to her and she wrote them down in a way that you could read them.

And special thanks to Reta Beall (a teacher from San Quentin and the seminary) for editing this book multiple times – even during the holiday season – and as always, putting aside all her other thesis work to get to my stuff immediately. I really owe my graduation from the seminary to her as she always edited my papers there as well.

Foreword

It is a pleasure to write this forward to William "Bill" Dew's autobiography. It is a story of God's intervention into his life and of the calling of Bill Dew unto the Lord.

I met Bill while serving as the National Director of the Contextualized Leadership Development Program of Golden Gate Baptist Theological Seminary The purpose of the program, originally known as Ethnic Leadership Development, was to provide ministry training for laity and those called to serve as church planters or pastors in the language of their birth, at places close to where they live, by qualified instructors, at a cost they could afford. Basically ELD/CLD provided a seminary education where people lived.

In 2006, Morris Curry, who was the Protestant Chaplain at San Quentin State Prison in the San Francisco Bay Area, contacted me. Chaplain Curry had a burden to train and disciple men who had become believers to serve the Lord in the "Incarcerated Church" and then outside the walls when they were paroled.

The CLD program began offering classes at San Quentin State Prison in the Fall of 2006. Two diplomas were offered: Diploma in Christian Ministry (24 hours credit) and an advanced diploma: Diploma in Theology (28 additional hours credit). These diplomas were designed for men and women who did not have a college degree. The instructors were volunteers who gave of their time and ministry. Each class was required to meet weekly for a minimum of two hours and fifty minutes for fifteen weeks. Textbooks were purchased with funds from churches, Sunday School classes, and believers from across North America. We had difficulties getting qualified instructors approved and textbooks inside the prison, and had to contend prison lockdowns and bad weather that caused classes to be cancelled. The Lord was faithful to the inmates and instructors as they answered his call.

I met Bill at New Student Orientation soon after he arrived at San Quentin, and then was an instructor for some of his classes. I was blessed to see Bill Dew's hunger to know and study God's Word. He had a lot of questions, doubts, and a growing faith. He was faithful in his attendance, studying, doing his homework and preparing for tests. William Dew began to have a Biblical filter that he began to run his ideas and plans through before he took action. It was a joy to observe the changes taking place in his life.

Bill completed the first CLD diploma and was working on his second when he asked me what was available for him to continue his education after completing the Diploma in Theology. I shared with him that GGBTS had a program whereby he could work on a Diploma of Educational Leadership or a Diploma in Theology without an earned college degree. I also mentioned that since he was over 30 years of age, if he maintained a 3.2 grade point on a 4.0 scale, he could be accepted as a master's student (by exception) after 20 hours of study and receive some credit for his CLD courses. This became William Dew's goal, which he achieved.

It has been a privilege to serve as Bill Dew's CLD instructor, counselor, friend, and, most of all, his brother in Christ. I pray for Bill, his wife, children, and ministry regularly. I commend this book to you.

C. Don Beall, Retired
Contextualized Leadership Development National Director
Golden Gate Baptist Theological Seminary

CHAPTER ONE

The Beginning of the Bruises

I have heard it said that one of the primary aims of our enemy, the devil, is to bruise every child from birth in such a way that he or she will never be able to function in the way God intended.

1 Peter 5:8 says that "Our enemy, the devil, prowls around like a roaring lion seeking who he may devour."

I have often wondered whether a troubled child is born or formed. Do the things people experience in life cause them to turn towards the dark side? It is an age old question—nurture or nature.

In my life, the first "bruise" I encountered was having an overly harsh father who was a strong disciplinarian. I was born into a normal, middle class family in rural Missouri. My father had a good job with Armor meats and ended up in the leadership of this company. His dad had been an alcoholic and was abusive to him, so it seems this behavior was a generational curse. My mother was a good stay-at-home mom who loved both my brother and me and cooked and looked after us well. We lived in a nice house and ate out often and were even members of the Freemasons' country club.

Maybe I tried to get my father's attention in negative ways, but I remember from an early age, I was always in trouble. I didn't have to go looking for it; trouble found me. Whether it was at school by not behaving in class or by stealing something I wanted, I was inevitably going to do something wrong, and my father was going to tan my hide for it. Sometimes it felt like he was beating me within an inch of my life for very small wrongs.

Looking back, I realize that my short attention span in class and being easily bored were probably proof that I was what today would be labeled an ADHD child. I was of above average intelligence, but I was not much interested in school. Once I was home, I performed all sorts of experiments and made my own toys by pulling apart other machinery. I clearly remember my father catching me riding my bike with the motor from his lawn mower attached. I was told to get it back on the lawn mower immediately, but I think he might have been secretly impressed with my mechanical prowess.

From early on in life, I could not delay gratification. I knew where my parents stored the Christmas gifts and would go into their bedroom when they weren't home, unwrap my gifts, and play with them. I once used half the chemicals in one of my science kit gifts and hoped they wouldn't realize it had been opened. Imagine my dismay when, after I had played with a nine band short wave radio that I knew was my gift, my father didn't give it to me for Christmas. I was caught because I couldn't admit I had already unwrapped it, so not giving it to me was how he taught me a lesson.

I know I had stresses in my young life, as I had developed an ulcer by 10 years of age. My mother would come to the elementary school every day with a milkshake that I would have to drink.

The second major bruise in my life was the death of my mother when I was only 11 years of age. I knew that something was going on as my mother was not at home with us for several weeks and we weren't allowed to visit her at the hospital. She called home and sounded very weak. Then her family would visit from out of town and I would see them crying, but nobody would tell my brother and I what was going on. When I asked if she going to die, I was told "no". She died of liver cancer when she was only 38 years old.

When the minister came over to the house to offer his condolences, he tried to tell me that God needed my mother. I cursed and screamed at him. I saw my mother in the coffin, and the body looked nothing like her, so I began to scream and ask where my mother was and what they had done to her. I had to be sedated for the funeral. My grandmother told me that I was the cause of her death and that if I had been a better boy, she wouldn't have died. How could anyone curse a child like that?

After my mom died, I went through numerous housekeepers who my dad employed to look after us. I could usually scare them off within a week by tormenting them. I was out of control – lighting stuff on fire, blowing things up, and sneaking out of the house. I remember that one of them was a drunk and she threw a mop handle at me as she was chasing me up the stairs, but I shut the door in time, and it left a big hole in the door.

I was sent away that summer to work on a relative's farm. We did hard labor all day in the hot sun, and I was made to work until I vomited. When I got home from that summer, my father had already met another lady and had moved her and her children into our house. At first she was very nice to my brother and me and would ask us what we would like for breakfast etc. As soon as my dad married her, however, she turned into the ugly stepmother who treated us badly when our dad wasn't around. She made us feel that we weren't welcome in our own home, and every one of my mother's pictures or keepsakes was thrown away.

Looking back, I still wonder where was God in this picture?

A counsellor asked me recently where I think Jesus was when my mother died. I thought long and hard about it, and I realized that He was right beside me during that terrible experience, holding my hand. We often think that God should save us from every negative experience, but that is not reality, and I now know that Jesus was right there with me, also feeling the grief that I felt at losing my mother.

The Bible tells us in Hebrews 13:5 that God will never leave us or forsake us, so even if we are feeling totally alone, we can know that God is there. If I keep an open mind when I look back on this experience and all the other times that came later, I realize that I can see God guiding and protecting me from myself or others and ordering my footsteps.

CHAPTER TWO

The Teenage Years and Hidden Bruises

Losing my mother and having my dad remarry so quickly really exacerbated my bad behavior. After the summer of my thirteenth year, I was sent to a school counselor. He tested students in the district for learning disabilities, and they wanted me tested, as I was doing so poorly at school. After testing me, however, he knew it wasn't my intelligence, but my attitude, that was the problem. He began having me over to his house on the weekends, and soon I was working at his testing center to help pay for the counseling sessions.

By age 13, I had already started stealing things, and I had my first encounter with the police. I had stolen a bike, and the police came to my house. My dad was furious with me and made me return the bike. My stepmother would get me to confide in her and then tell my Dad about the things I had stolen.

Finally, when I was 14, my stepmother gave my father an

ultimatum after I had stolen a go-cart. One of us had to go – me or her. My father chose her, and I was sent to live with the counselor full time. He became my guardian and started to isolate me from my family, playing on my feelings that they didn't care for me. He would get me to tear up the checks my father sent for my birthday and make me not want to see him. I saw very little of my family between the ages of 14 and 18. My father finally came to see me and told me they were moving to Phoenix, Arizona, and he said that I could go with them if I wanted, but my stepmother was sitting behind him, glaring at me. I decided to sacrifice myself, believing my family was better off without me. This decision also justified my anger and kept it boiling.

During the time I spent with the counselor/guardian and his family, he started to abuse me. First he tried to sexually abuse me when I was only 14. When he wasn't successful and I began to date girls, he got furiously angry, and the physical abuse started. He would beat on me until he broke his knuckles. This abuse went on for years until I began to fight back. I broke his nose once, and that just made him madder. This was a very dark time in my life.

While I was living there, I started going to a Baptist youth group to meet some girls. I pretended that I was interested in God and even made a public "decision" and was baptized. However, in truth I had very little interest in religion and was still mad that God had allowed my mother to die and my life to go to pieces after her death.

At this time, I saw God step into the picture of my life. The minister of the church came to see me at home and said that while on a trip overseas, God had told him I was only pretending and I wasn't really a Christian. He told me that I was mad at God and explained why I felt that way. I was so amazed that God knew me by name and knew my problems that I prayed with him and became a true believer.

When I look back on this time, I question myself. Is this the only way God could have stepped into my life – by leaving me with this sexual predator who forced me to go to church with threats and acts of violence? Could I not have found God in any other church? Did my mother have to die so I could find redemption? At the time, these questions were too hard to answer, so I put God on the back burner. No one could answer me, so I knew I would have to go to the source at some point to get my questions answered. Back then, I had a desire to learn more, and felt I should someday go to a Bible college and learn about God and how He works.

I got my first car at the age of 15 and started working on it in my time off. I also had my first serious girlfriend, Betsy. At 18, I found out she was sleeping around with other guys. Her behavior gave me a second impression that women could not be trusted or that they would always leave me, a feeling that stuck with me for most of my life.

From junior high until my first semester of high school, I frequently skipped school. I would go hunting with my pellet gun down at the creek – or if I saw anything that needed shooting or lighting on fire, I would do it. I did enjoy lighting a good campfire and a couple of them got away, but fortunately they didn't cause any fatalities.

After I moved in with Dr. P (for pervert), the school designed a program for me. Since I was ditching school anyway, they allowed me to take the afternoon off, and I would work at the De Paul University testing center in the afternoons. I would help my guardian test the special needs students and would tutor them. I also instructed the graduate students who were working on their Master's in Special Education degree on how to do the testing. I was even offered a scholarship to stay at the university and get my degree. If only I could have seen into my future, I would have made a different decision and taken that chance.

At this point in my life, I knew that God was real, but there was a serious disconnect. My guardian would abuse me and then force me to go to church on Sunday. I wanted to believe that Christianity was real, but from what I was observing in my own life, it seemed that the bad people who claimed to be Christians appeared to get away with what they were doing. This man was able to work at the university as a topnotch professor, but I could only get into the trades.

Yet I know, just as the scripture says, that God works all things together for our good, according to his good purpose. Even if bad things were done *to* me and some of them were not my fault, God uses every experience in our lives to perfect us into the image of His son, Jesus Christ.

I also know that I was never punished for many things I did wrong, so in the scheme of things, I am probably still behind.

CHAPTER THREE

My Life of Crime

The things I write in this chapter are not done to glorify my crimes, but to show the incredible grace of God in my life. Although I was completely willful and went my own way, His love and grace never left me, and He continually drew me back to Him.

My first real offence was strong-armed robbery. I happened to be in the company of a client who I was tutoring and who I hung around with sometimes. We were going out one night for dinner. He was walking ahead of me, and as I walked around a corner, I saw him holding up a guy with a switchblade, so I clicked my knife open to support him. He split the money with me, so I was an accomplice, although I hadn't planned it. The De Paul law clinic defended us, and I was fortunate that I received only probation this time.

When I was 18, I was finally allowed to move out of my counselor's home. He wouldn't give me all my belongings, so I went back to the house and took a stuffed shark off the wall that I had caught while fishing (this act was eventually ruled a felony theft). I got a job working as a roofer, but I started getting into trouble over the next year. This period of my life was when I started my life of crime.

I was off the hook and out of control. I wrote bad checks, burglarized my boss's house, committed theft, rode with a motorcycle gang, got into fights, and got high on acid, all while I was roofing. I had multiple charges against me, at least four of which were felonies, not to mention the multiple times I was charged for carrying a concealed weapon. I think I stopped counting after 27 times. The judge dropped some charges and I pled guilty to others, so I was fortunate to be given only a year in jail with work release.

While I was serving my time, I would get out of jail early (around 5 a.m.) and start walking until friends would pick me up. I sold pot to buy a car and set up work for my two buddies and myself. One of them would drive my car and pick me up, but I would often have to walk five to seven miles before they made it out of bed to fetch me. These are my fondest memories of time alone with God and his communication with me. He promised things and delivered over and over. He told me to start my own roofing company even though I was in jail, and I did so well my probation officer asked for a job later on when I became successful. I was about 20. I then bought into my boss' company that had been owned by a mob connected guy. We had to start buying our supplies from their contractors, who would send us work in exchange for kickbacks. I did all this while I was incarcerated.

After I finished this jail term, I bought my first Harley and went riding with other roofers who were in a motorcycle gang called the Freedom Riders. (My talks with God were paused and I would only catch Jimmy Swaggart on TV in the early morning hours after the bars closed). We would go into small towns on the weekends and take over the whole town. The inhabitants, even the police, would leave, and we would create mayhem. I would be in a few bar fights with the bikers, and we would get jumped by rednecks. However, I saw lots of gratuitous violence that I eventually could not be a part of. The bikers would pick on hippies who were selling drugs and would beat them up and take their drugs when we went into the forest preserves in and around Chicago.

One time I received a load of bad pot, so I cancelled the check I used to buy it. Two or three of the criminals who had sold me the pot came after me and kicked in my door, so I shot them. I shot one in the chest, and I didn't know whether he was dead or alive. I hit the other one in the groin area. I was charged and went to court, but the case was dismissed as self-defense as they had 2 x 4 wooden clubs with them, which they left at the scene. This was another time where I saw God step in. My parole officer was sitting in the courtroom just waiting for me to be violated so he could take me back to jail. Fortunately, the guy didn't die, but I was lucky as I could have been dead or charged with murder/manslaughter or GBH.

I wrote bad checks whenever I needed money. I created fake businesses and wrote checks back and forth between the businesses. A would pay B, B would pay C, and while these checks were floating around, I would withdraw all the money and start again with new banks. In those days, people didn't need much in the way of ID. One time I had a bank president call me in to ask me how I did it all, as it was such an elaborate scheme.

Around this time, I met the woman I would later marry. I met Sharon in a bar and lived with her until she was pregnant with our first child, Christeena, and then I married her. This was not really a love match, but I saw friends around me hooking up with significant others, so I felt it was time I did as well. She showed up often enough to the bar, and I thought, well, she is always around and I could get my needs met whenever I wanted. She was also not sharp enough to know what I was doing to earn money.

Unfortunately, Sharon was a drunk, and during our ten-year marriage, she went on drunken binges and left Christeena with me. Through her brother-in-law and some mutual friends, I got mixed up with the Chicago mob. I began building a business and criminal empire. I was able to use the mob lawyers to get me off on any of my crimes.

I found out my new suppliers for roofing materials were taking a kickback through double invoicing or for houses that didn't exist. I was very mad. The mob lawyers said it was a conflict of interest as the suppliers also worked for the mob, so they couldn't help me. As a result, I filed for bankruptcy. I collected all the accounts receivable money and left Al Capone's nephew, among others, with the bills. I was informed not to leave town without finishing the roofs. They warned me and they had hired a hit man to get rid of me. I only finished a few, but then I was blackballed in Chicago, so my business was small and I could get materials from only certain lumber yards and home improvement stores, which seriously limited what I could do.

The biggest builder in the Chicago area had previously given me lots of work and was a buddy, but he told me that he had a wife and kids and couldn't afford to help me any longer. As a result of these issues, my business became very small with only a handful of roofers working for me.

One time, my sister-in-law was screwing around with one of my men, so her husband E, who was also my partner, and I went to get our tools from the back of one of the trucks. While we were there, E saw the guy and pulled his gun, so he and his gang all pulled their guns and told us to get out of there. I told them if they wanted to play it that way, then they could get what was coming. I then built a large pipe bomb using black powder, which was rated at six to eight sticks of dynamite, and threw it under the gas tank of the truck for effect. The truck blew up into the air in a flaming ball of fire.

By the time we were nearing home, there was a stakeout on the highway, so we had to ditch the vehicle and go through a restaurant, out the back, and make our way to E's father's house. He was the manager of a nearly abandoned housing apartment project. We were holed up there all night while the SWAT teams came in from all neighboring suburbs and all the buildings were evacuated. E accidentally shot through the roof, so they backed off. The police thought we meant business and they would get shot or blown up. I found out later that Sharon, my wife, had called the police and told them who blew up the truck after her brother called her and told her what had happened.

I had a Jewish mafia lawyer who I used for anything outside Cook County. Because the victim was the president of the local bike club and he, along with his friends, would beat up anyone who passed, I was considered somewhat of a hero for taking them on. The police even gave me a nickname, "The Friendly Arsonist," as I always looked clean cut and was polite.

My lawyer bribed the D.A., who was retiring, to take $5000

to give a recommendation of probation. When this happened, the judge questioned the police officers, who were clearly trying to minimize the case, and then he got mad at the D.A. He said he was leaving the courtroom and when he came back he didn't want to see any of us there and he wouldn't touch it without giving us at least 30 days of jail time. When we came back to court, the lawyer told the judge I would serve 90 days of jail time, along with five years' probation, and pay for a new truck for the victim. He had to fight fiercely with the judge to get him to accept this offer, and he threatened that he could hold the case up all day. The judge agreed to this plan, so I did the 90 days, and then shortly thereafter I was called out of town to pick Sharon up in Florida where she was living with her mother and getting drunk. She would leave Christeena with her mother, which cramped her mother's style.

During this time, I had been suffering a lot from a bleeding ulcer. I had also been crying out to God to release me from this terrible marriage. I was sure my wife was cheating on me, but I didn't have proof. One Sunday I went to church with her. I went down to the prayer line for my ulcer, and the pastor prayed for me and told me I was healed, which I doubted because of the incredible pain I had in my stomach. That night, Sharon went out on one of her drinking binges. While dealing with the baby, whom she had left behind, I called the grandmother to come and pick her up. I was praying to God that if I had proof of adultery, I could divorce Sharon. Right away, the phone rang. It was a friend of mine who had recently got saved, and he felt compelled to confess to me that he had been sleeping with my wife and he was now alarmed at some of her behaviors. She lied to him, saying that I had thrown her out, but she was still driving my truck so he knew that wasn't the truth. He was very scared that I would hurt him, as he knew how violent I could be. Since he had the guts to tell me, I forgave him immediately.

Right away, I felt my stomach getting worse. I started throwing up and noticed there was a lot of blood in the toilet. That repeated a few times, so I called the hospital and they told me to come in. On the way, I felt the Lord tell me that I was healed and could go back home, but I couldn't take a chance, so I still went to the hospital and was ready for a long overdue surgery. When I got there, I was sent for tests. The doctor came out and was very angry with me. He said, "Not only is there no ulcer or bleeding now or tonight, there never has been." He thought I was some kind of weirdo and was wasting his time. I told him that I had been at that hospital the month before, and they would have records. I told him I had been at church that night, and God had told the pastor I was healed. He said that would be the only explanation. I was so happy that it had worked and God was real in my life, but healing of my ulcer had little effect on my behavior.

Several of my trials were coming up at the same time for various crimes I had done, and my lawyer kept asking for continuances. He called in favors to get me one last continuance and told me I needed to get out of town. During this time, I had warrants out for various nefarious activities, so I got out of Dodge and started roofing in Florida.

Sometimes it is like the Kenny Rogers song – you've got to know when to fold 'em, and it was time to go. I am glad I listened to this wise advice and got out before I was dead or back in prison.

CHAPTER FOUR

The Florida and Texas Years

When I left Chicago, I drove down to Pace, Florida, near Pensacola. I rented a trailer that was on some land and started roofing for the local roofing company. I worked my way up in the company to become their key roofer.

During this time, the KKK tried to recruit me. I went to several rallies, but I didn't like what they were doing so much as to join. They were big in that town and almost ran it. Any time they were put in jail for gun charges or something else from the Feds, the local guys would let them run wild, and they would put child molesters in with them to get beat up or killed. I witnessed this first hand, so to speak, on multiple occasions.

My wife Sharon told the police I was wanted in Chicago, so one day they came to get me while I was in my trailer. I thought it was the Chicago mob guys when two guys wearing suits and driving an unmarked car pulled up. I grabbed my .45 and aimed it at the driver. The passenger got down and the driver rolled out of the car, by which time I realized they were police and not the mob. They got so mad at me and told me they nearly shot me. I think they were mad because I had the drop on them, but as soon as I realized they were cops, I put my gun away and had my hands in the air. They tried to tell me they could have killed me as their guns were more accurate than mine . . . shoulda, woulda, coulda. (They were right; mine was a snub nosed 45).

We had to wait at the police station until my record came in. I told them it was all a big mistake. Then the teletype (how it was done in the old days) machine started going, and they saw my name on it. The first couple of charges I tried to explain away, but when around a dozen pages had come out of the machine, I shut up.

They held me on warrants out of Chicago and put out one of their own for being a felon carrying a concealed weapon. While I was in the jail there, I witnessed a couple of people being beaten to death by the Klan in the tank next door, so I told myself I needed to get out of there quick.

Every time she came to see me, Sharon told me that the detective on the case was trying to get her to snitch on other criminals to get me out. I told her to tell the guy that she didn't know anything about them. I did, however, and I had used that knowledge before with the Chicago police to get out of trouble. I assured her that the detective would eventually have to call me down to his office, and he did.

God had told me during this time that all my Chicago warrants would be taken care of within 30 days. I kept telling Sharon it would all be okay, and I was witnessing to other people about it. For this detective to use me, all the other charges would have to be amended and changed to local charges only.

They had to be taken out of the national computer and made local only, which meant they would not extradite me, and that is exactly what happened.

At that time, they had a big problem with cocaine being smuggled in. The detective thought he could use me as a snitch, so I told him that I knew what he had been asking my wife and that I had done it before. With my Chicago accent, the drug smugglers would just think I was a buyer, and I had the criminal connections I could use as a reference that I was a bad guy. He went for it, and within a few weeks I was out of jail.

He gave me the name of the person with whom he wanted me to make contact at a certain bar. He had me sign all the papers and threatened to hunt me down if I took off. I got in my car, went home, packed up, and left town. I had already rented a U-Haul trailer the night before. The car caught on fire in the middle of town with the trailer on it, and I thought for sure I was caught, as it was a little town. I unhooked the trailer from the car and a few friends helped me push it into the parking lot of a motel that was nearby. I caught a cab and went down the road where I knew a car was for sale. I bought it and got a trailer hitch from the U-Haul people, and I was soon back in business and heading for Texas.

I arrived in the Dallas/Fort Worth area soon after a big hailstorm had hit Fort Worth, and there was lots of work for roofers. I only had the Chevy Biscayne, an old six cylinder from the 70s, that I had driven there, but I told the Sears people that I had multiple trucks and six workers ready to go. They started giving me contracts, and I worked so hard that soon I was in business. I called a couple of my friends from Chicago who were roofers to come down and help me. I also put an ad in the paper for local guys with their own trucks and I was able to pull it off. I was making lots of money but blowing it just as quickly.

Work became competitive after the hailstorm work was done. I started drifting around in Texas looking for other work. I moved on to near Houston but found out the pay scale was too low, so I moved down to Victoria, Texas, where I knew a builder was setting up new projects. I told the main builder I was all that and a bag of chips, but he asked me where all my guys were. I told him they were on their way. I did have a nice little dump truck that I had picked up while I was in Fort Worth. He had me bid on the project, and I gave him a good price. I started roofing after telling him I was waiting for the guys to arrive. Of course, there were no guys on their way. I put an ad in the paper and got a local guy to help me. He was older than dirt, but I was so desperate I thought I would let him up on the roof, and it wasn't far to fall. That guy could roof like greased lightning. He just happened to be in town, living at his sister's house, and he was a drunk. He was worthless when he got drunk, but the rest of the time, he was hard to stay ahead of.

I did several bank fraud scams when work was slow. I had split up with my wife Sharon in Texas, and she had gone back to Chicago, but then her mother called me and asked me to take her back. She was an alcoholic and went on binges. One time while she was with me in Victoria, she went to the CPS office, left Christeena there, and split town. The CPS worker came out to the project and said I had to come into their office. They said Sharon told them she was just going out to get cigarettes, but she never came back – that was the afternoon before. I had to take Christeena, but I still had to work. I would take her to work with me and set up the back of the truck like a big play pen. Sharon came back to town a bit later and took Christeena back to Chicago. This happened two different times, but I always took her back. I became known as "Captain Save a Ho."

I finally moved to Phoenix, partly to be near my dad, but also because that was where the work was. I still didn't see much of him because of the step mom, and we were both busy working. Wife Sharon followed me to Phoenix to say she was pregnant with my second daughter, Jenny. Sharon went back and forth. She would go to her mom until her mom got sick of her and sent her back. She would call the police to try to get me in trouble. One time she pulled my gun on me and tried to shoot it, so I slapped her. Another time, when our pastor came to visit and he was near the front door, she started yelling for help and saying "leave me alone" and "don't hit me" when I was nowhere near her. I pulled her inside, and she fell over a chandelier on the floor. She filed domestic violence charges on me for various things like this. The pastor told the police he had seen the whole thing and I hadn't touched her. He explained that it was an accident, but they didn't care. My record was what counted now.

I desperately wanted to change and tried to attend the Assemblies of God Bible College. I was still passing bad checks during this time when funds were low. This is another time I really saw Jesus step in. An Italian detective from the Scottsdale fraudulent schemes division arrested me after a stakeout at my house. I had returned to pick up some medicine I accidently left behind when leaving town just ahead of the police. He told me he had all the facts and bad checks and knew all about the bank scam I was in the middle of. It was up to 50,000 to 75,000 per bank at every major bank in the Phoenix area at that time. He said they had been watching me for a long time and had lots of evidence. He showed me the photos he had. At this stage, I would get 25 to life if convicted.

During the questioning, I was kind of talking to myself and saying, "What the hell is wrong with me? I don't need the money. I'm a Christian, so why can't I stop?" I told him I had tried and tried but just couldn't go straight. He told me that he was a Christian and that I was doing it wrong. He said, "You don't try and try; you give it to Jesus and let Him change you." It finally made sense to me. He asked me if I would sign a confession. I said yes, as long as I could get one last time with my wife and daughter to say goodbye. After I signed it, he took my shoelaces and put me back in the cellblock. I fell on my knees and prayed, not that God would get me out of it, but that He would help me through it and look after my wife and kids. I then felt at peace and lay down on the bunk. The detective came back to my cell, threw my shoelaces at me, and said, "Get out of here." He told me he was too late to get me into a preliminary hearing, so he was giving me a break, hoping maybe I would finally get my life together.

I was given several breaks in life. A guy I met owned a roofing company, and he asked me to take the exam for him to become a contractor. His wife managed an apartment complex that had a government subsidy and she handpicked the people who could go there. I took the exam for him and was given a nice three-bedroom apartment in this complex for next to nothing.

I was attending a local Assemblies of God at the time and

going to their seminary of sorts to get ordained and certified to preach. One night we had a female evangelist come to preach, and I was asked to be an usher and help catch people when she was praying for them. I was very skeptical of those who were falling over, being "slain in the Spirit." The evangelist called my wife Sharon out of the audience, prayed over her, and prophesied over her. Then she turned to me and said, "You are her husband, aren't you?" She told me to come up to the front, and she started to read my mail. I knew that she couldn't possibly know about me, and it was very embarrassing, as not everyone in the congregation knew my story. She said I was struggling with demonic oppression and I needed to get free. She said she would pray for me and I would get temporary relief, but I needed to find someone who was an expert in that area.

After she prayed for me, I staggered backwards and felt like I had just had a huge hit of dope. In the next few days, I went around to a few places to see if someone could help me. A few would come to the house and pray for me, but I felt that nothing had changed. I finally found a Christian psychologist who talked to me and gave me a prayer and ritual to go through every day. I didn't think it would help, but I tried it anyway. I asked him how long it would take, and he told me that I would know when it was done.

One night I started hearing things in the house, and I thought I was going nuts. I called him up, and he got all excited and said that was what we wanted to happen and to keep it up. Later I told him that I wasn't going crazy as my young daughter Christeena was also hearing and seeing the same things I was and could describe them to me. He got even more excited and said, "You're almost there; now you've got them on the run." I suspected that he didn't often have those kinds of results.

Another night I was praying and going over the ritual. I kept hearing a voice in my mind to go and get rid of the tapes. I felt impressed to stop what I was doing and look for any tapes that were in the house. I looked straight across from me, and on the bookcase I saw a cassette tape by AC/DC, Highway to Hell, that I had never seen before. I went outside to throw it on the BBQ, just outside the door. When I came back inside and closed the door, it flew back open. This happened several times, and it kept getting harder and harder to close the door each time. It finally took all my weight to get the door closed and locked, and when I looked out the window, there was nothing there. As it turned out, that was the final straw that broke the camel's back, and I felt free from demonic oppression. I finally had a slight toe hold on my temper.

A few years later, I met a guy at my apartment building who would get stolen goods, so I began to sell the stuff at the swap meet. He was a drug addict and had previously swapped the goods for drugs. I offered cash. He was a painter and would scout out places to burglarize. I finally ended up doing burglaries with him. Sometimes, I would fly to California for weekends and do burglaries with this friend who had moved there after he was paroled back to California to his parents' house. I had custody of my two children at this time. I would send my kids to Sunday school even if I didn't attend church. One day I went to pick up the kids, but there was no one there, and it turned out wife Sharon had come and picked up the kids and taken them back to Chicago. We divorced when my second daughter, Jenny, was three.

CHAPTER FIVE

The Arizona/California years

I would go back and forth to church during this time. I tried to clean up my act on my own and was still not taking the advice the detective gave me, to give all my issues to Jesus.

Around this time, my burglary partner had a sister, Karen, who was rescued from a local Satanic cult. He asked me to be her bodyguard to stop them from recapturing her. She had been held by them against her will. They made snuff films, and she was going to be one of the ones featured in them. I let her stay in one of my rooms. The cult was afraid of me, as I brought in my mob buddy and his crew to scare the bejesus out of them. They wanted to kill them, but we just wanted them scared.

Of course, Captain Save a Ho hadn't learned his lesson. I thought I could rescue someone when my own life was a mess. Karen and I started sleeping together, and soon she was pregnant with my first son, William Dew III. During this time, she would relapse into drugs and the cult people would be waiting. They hooked her back into their cult ways and even convinced her to sacrifice our son. She had already done this with a fetus, and they were brainwashing her into doing it with a live baby. I found some books on this subject and was so incensed that I warned her I would cut the baby out of her and take it to the hospital if she even thought of doing something like this.

Around this time, I started taking Karen to church. Although she was on her best behavior, the pastors could see right through her. They told me that there was demonic oppression and our house was infested with demons and that someone was allowing this. I tried to get the pastors and even a priest to come over to the house and cleanse it, but they all felt they were out of their depth.

One night while Karen and I were arguing, she went into the bathroom. When she came back out, she ran at me, and I saw her whole appearance start to morph in an indescribable way, like a demon was taking her over – and I was in fear of my life. It felt like an eight-foot demon was inside the house and was hunched over just to fit in it. When she noticed that I was looking afraid, she glanced at a mirror and saw herself, and she went running back into the bathroom.

We were both on drugs during this time, though I was more off and on than she was. I would use for a weekend but be clean during the week so I could work. I was still roofing, painting, and doing some burglary on the side with her brother. She was slamming speed while pregnant with our son. After he was born, she would neglect him to get high, and I would come home to find the baby in a filthy diaper and no food in the house.

Once when I was in jail, I was presented with papers that said they had found my son with filthy diapers, poop all over the walls, and no food in the house. I got served with "failure to protect" papers, as I wasn't protecting my son from his mother.

A few months later, Karen was pregnant again with our daughter. She continued to use speed. My daughter Sarah was born positive for drugs, and they were going to take her away. I blamed the doctor for giving Karen opiates in her cough syrup, and so we were able to take Sarah home.

This was a time of complete chaos in my life. I had no control over this woman who relapsed time after time. Not only would she relapse with the drugs but with cult activity. Our home was full of demons from all the stuff she would bring into the house. When I found all the stuff for performing spells, I flipped out and cleaned out the house, and it turned into a huge issue. She called the police and had me cited for domestic violence.

She tried to kill me on more than one occasion. She tried to run me down with a car and a truck, hit me over the head with cast iron skillets, and shoot me with a gun. One time, I woke up to hear a gun clicking. I jumped up, took the cylinder out so she couldn't fire the gun, and left the house. I was picked up not much later and arrested for assault with a firearm. I tried to explain to them what I had done, but she had turned it around on me. No one believed me that she would try to kill me, but she later actually did kill the guy she was married to after me. She held a satanic ritual, shot him in the knees, and let him bleed out over a long period of time because he was going to leave her. God had, once again, saved my life.

While I was in jail, she liquidated everything I owned and turned it into drugs. She also neglected the children while she was getting high. Her brother told me that she had a boyfriend while I was locked up, so I filed for divorce.

Not long after, she was arrested and went to jail, and CPS told me that I had to take the children. She continually failed the reunification chances that she got. I felt completely unqualified, as I was freshly out of jail and in a halfway house. CPS told me they would help me, so I had to quickly find a place to live, furnish it, and be ready for a house inspection.

All the women who I knew from recovery helped me get the apartment and furnish it. They helped me look after the children. During these years, my ex-wife's sister would come and help with the children. She was married to a cop, but she suggested that we get together. I told her to go back to her husband and from then on, she hated me. She got her cop husband to raid me on several occasions.

My wife's whole family was full of demonic oppression, and the mother was the worst enabler of them all. They would cover up for each other. The brother was my partner in crime, and the mother would help hide the stolen goods. I finally knew that I had to get away from this family altogether.

When I first got Billy and Sarah, I was in school taking classes for drug and alcohol counseling. I got aid for dependent children as I was a single parent, so that paid for the whole thing. I had women in the housing complex babysit while I went to school.

I had no real idea how to look after young children, and they were running riot over me. By the time I got them, they had been abused in the foster home and were used to time-outs that could last all day. They had also been whipped for any small problems, and their health issues were not addressed. When I picked them up from the foster home, the first stop I had to make was the pediatrician. Sarah had been giving off a terrible odor for months and was supposed to have been taken to the doctor but had not been. It turned out that she had a putrefied growth up her nose, from some small toy that had been pushed up there, and it had turned septic. The doctor had to use long forceps to get it out.

There was no way I could discipline them when they wanted to get wild. It seemed like they knew when I was getting the house ready for the CPS inspections, and they would go crazy and the house would look like a bomb had hit it. CPS knew I was in trouble, so they suggested sending out a behavior modification specialist.

They sent out Rodney, a young social worker, who showed me how to give the carrot and stick treatment. I put a chart high up on the wall, with every day of the week, and I would put chores on each day, with simple tasks, like eat your breakfast, make your bed, go to school etc. They were always able to achieve their gold stars. If they had had a bad day, I always came up with an extra activity on Saturday so they could redeem themselves and then we would go shopping at the dollar store. They could get any toy they wanted.

When I noticed they couldn't decide which toy they wanted, I went back and bought them all. I stuck them high up on the wall in the dining room and put their chart underneath. They would drool every day as they were eating, talking about which toy they were going to get. Sometimes they would argue about whether it was a boy or girl toy and who was going to get it. This was old-fashioned bribery, but it worked like a charm. Rodney said he had never seen anyone do such an elaborate job of it, and he was impressed. He called it positive reinforcement.

After I got out of prison and before I got the kids back, I had been sent to rehab, as I had relapsed immediately on getting out. I met Donna, a younger woman, in rehab. I knew that she liked me and she would come and help with the kids. She finally moved in with me, as I desperately needed help. We decided to break ties with everyone in California. I had gotten off parole, so I was free to leave the area. We decided to head for my hometown in Missouri.

Young Bill

Jenny

Jenny and Christeena

Christeena

Young Billy and Sarah

Jenny aged 19

William Dew III

Sarah

Bill with young Hannah and Elijah

Bill Graduating

Bill and Jill's wedding

Seeing Hannah and Elijah for the first time in many years

Christeena

Family pic with Hannah and Elijah

Elijah Hannah Billy

Bill, Jill and Elijah

CHAPTER SIX

California Years

I had completed most of the custody battle with my ex regarding the children, and she had to make only one more appearance. I decided, however, to just take the kids and leave and give them a new start, so Donna and I got all our stuff together, rented a U-Haul, and headed for Missouri with my two children, Billy and Sarah. They were about three and four at this time.

Not long after we settled in our new home, the local police served me with a warrant out of California and arrested me. The charge was that I had violated my parole and had kidnapped my children from daycare. I bonded out of jail, but I still had to face the charges.

The clerk of the court called me and told me that the D.A. from California was there on an ex-parte hearing and that I had 15 minutes to appear in court if I wanted to defend myself. I rushed to court, bringing the paperwork to show the judge that the ones pressing charges were lying – the judge was furiously angry and threw the D.A. out of the courtroom.

After a while, the D.A. got a federal order to take the children back to the jurisdiction of California. They said they still had final jurisdiction; this was because my ex-wife would not attend the hearings and kept getting a continuance. They charged me with custodial interference, and because of my record (the three strike law), they were trying to wobble it up to a felony. They took my children.

I was still in Missouri trying to fight extradition, but finally I heard that a warrant from California had come through and I should just go back and surrender myself and fight the court case there. As a result, I got on a bus, traveling two or three days. My mind was in turmoil, and I felt like running. A guy sitting behind me on the bus was a part of the Christian motorcycle club. He delivered motorhomes, driving them to their destination and then taking the bus back to where he lived. He said that on every journey, God would have him speak to someone on the bus, and I knew this time it was me. I told him the whole story, and he strongly advised me to keep going to California and face the charges, reassuring me that God would see me through. I was so angry at God, as I had been trying to do the right thing and I hadn't done anything wrong that time, and here I was again, maybe heading back to prison.

I was still going to fight it, as I felt I was innocent, but the judge called my lawyer up for a sidebar conference and wanted to know why I wasn't taking the deal of four years at 80 percent to serve. She told my lawyer she was giving me one last chance to reconsider and that she would strike me out if I didn't take the deal. It was a hard decision, but I could not afford to go away for 25 years to life. She told me I would be thankful to her later on. I took the deal, and I did end up being thankful because while I was serving my time, I met guys who said they had already been in prison longer than they would have had to serve if they had just taken the deal.

When I was arrested in California and was in the Receiving Center, a guy knocked on the door. He was one of my buddies who was a drug counselor and working at the prison. They had a pilot program for the state, and I was able to get into the program. While I was in prison, I was able to facilitate groups, give seminars, and do classes on relapse prevention. I realized that God had changed the rotten dynamics around by giving me a chance to start working in the field and adding this experience to my resume. I was also able to get some deep inner healing. It turned out to be a very productive time.

In the meantime, Donna was pregnant with our daughter, Hannah. We had joined a church in St. Joseph, Missouri (Word of Life with Brian Zahnd). Those people really acted like the church when I was arrested. They supported us in every way they could think of. They helped with things around the house and gave her groceries. Donna came home once to find a pastor mowing our lawn; she said he looked to be about 90 years old. She had been able to get work for a while, but then her grandfather in California convinced her to go and live with them. They said they would help her look after our daughter.

She had a probation violation out for her in California and her step-grandmother later turned her in. We always suspected that she wanted our daughter, Hannah, for herself. Donna got the issue straightened out, spent a month in jail, and got out with time served.

Since I was in prison, I couldn't see her or my newborn

daughter. Just before I got out, her grandparents told her that I couldn't come back to their house, so she went to the Salvation Army and got a bunch of furniture, rented an apartment, and picked me up at the prison. The parole department had to approve the apartment first. My daughter was very shy with me, as she was now three years of age and had never met me.

I got out of prison one day and the very next day I was in school, resuming my classes to become a drug counselor. I would watch Hannah during the day, while Donna worked. She had a good job at the county. After she came home from work, I attended school from 6 to 10 at night. I would have to come home each evening and make a pitcher of margaritas, just to get through it. Donna told me that she hadn't waited three years for me to come home and be a drunk. I told her to just give me a few weeks to settle down, as I didn't even like alcohol.

I had been in school for a semester when they had some mock interviews as part of our program. I was interviewed by a local rehabilitation shelter. Not long after, my professor told me that the lady who ran the shelter was so impressed with my interview that she would like to hire me part time. Soon I was going to school and working part time. Because I was a student, Hannah was able to go to the college daycare.

Pretty soon I was doing more and more hours, and then they put me in charge of the whole case management department. The operations department looked after the rules and the whole operation of the place. When the lady in charge died, the Chairman of the Board decided I should be put in charge of the whole place. There were about 125 residents at the shelter, and I had to manage their day-to-day operations and case management. They decided I had enough expertise to do both.

Donna was now pregnant with our second son, Elijah. After he was born, I took him to the daycare at the school where Hannah was in pre-school. I was ready to do the last class of the school, which was the practicum. We were supposed to use some of the students at the school in the shelter, and I would manage them, but somehow it never happened and no one signed off on my practicum, so I am still one class short of a drug counseling degree. I did, however, sign off on the Master's students sent to us for their psychology degree.

While I was still working at the shelter, I started DGW (Doing God's Work) ministries and rented a gang infested, rundown apartment complex. I used it to create a 90-bed shelter that provided transitional, sober living housing. I was run off my feet, both working at the rehab shelter and then running one of my own. To manage, I would find a person who had personal authority (a natural leader) and then vest him or her with authority to run the place. Finally, I had enough of working at the shelter, as the figurehead person, who was a nun, became very picky and objected to me doing my own personal business. She would make ridiculous rules about smoking for 10 minutes on the hour, and she would report each person who didn't comply. It was nit-picking, and I couldn't handle it anymore, so I quit.

I then concentrated on my own shelter, and I beefed up the therapeutic side of it. I was in my element, working this job, as I loved helping people, and I liked working out problems.

During this time, my second daughter came from Chicago to live with me. Jenny was trying to get her nursing license. She had been taking drugs in Chicago, but I never saw her take drugs when she was with me. One day, Donna found some heroin in the bathroom and became really upset. She gave me an ultimatum: Jenny had to go or she would. She also filed a restraining order against my daughter. I believed in tough love at that time, so I told my daughter she had to leave, but I had a motorhome in the backyard that I kept open for her with hookups to water and electricity.

Finally, her mother wanted her back in Chicago, so I took her to the plane and sent her off. She wasn't back there for long when I got the phone call that nearly destroyed me. She had overdosed on heroin and was found dead in a sleazy apartment building in Chicago. I could not handle this news and felt the heavy burden of guilt that I had sent her back to her death. I have to say, I am still not over this, even to this day, but during her time with me, she had given her life to Jesus. When she lived with me as a small child she would often be down at the altar call, and I knew that she was safe with Him.

Toxic mold showed up in the apartments. Because I insisted that the owner of the property fix this problem and fulfil his contract, we ended up in a three-year long civil court battle. The last time I saw him, I told him that he shouldn't be treating homeless people that way and that God would not be happy with him. He just laughed and said there is no God. At the next hearing, I was told his side needed a continuance, as his car had stalled on the freeway and had been run into by another car. He and his wife were dead. Everyone looked at me like I had had him whacked. I knew God had intervened, but I still felt guilty.

In the end, the family turned the building back into a normal apartment complex. All the homeless people were put out on the street. I had put $20,000 aside to rent another place. When I went to get it from our bank account, it was gone.

My wife had spent it on drugs. I flipped out and told her that because of her, all those homeless people were now back on the street. The irony is that my now ex-wife has been working for years, on the night shift, at the very same shelter that these people were sent to. She has never been able to escape that life.

This event led to a series of discoveries that were the beginning of the end of life as we all knew it. I came to find out that the taxes, both personal and for the ministry, had not been paid or had been filed fraudulently. All accounts had been drained and loans had been taken out. Credit cards were unpaid. I set it up so I could watch my wife's history and find out where she was buying her drugs. I soon learned she was buying from online pharmacies and having them delivered to her work or to her friends' homes. Strange things started happening. Her boss followed her home when she was too high to drive, she fell out from drugs while on school trips, and she drove with the kids in the car when she was high.

When I had met her in the rehab, she was there because of criminal behavior. She came from a home with an addicted mother and had been declared incorrigible by the court. However, she had straightened out in the program and was put on part time staff, so by the time we got together, she was functioning as a normal person who held down an important job. I knew that she had crossed the line a few times, as she was working as a paralegal and her friend was also a paralegal and notary and they would sign off on documents for each other. I told her she couldn't be doing it as they would think, due to my criminal background, that I had put her up to it.

By this time, we had been together for around 10 years, and most of the time she was a good partner and mother. However, just before it all came crashing down, she started acting out. She wanted to get a stomach bypass, as she was very overweight, and I was against it. She had the surgery anyway, and she ran into complications and bled excessively because she was already hooked on opiates and didn't tell the doctors. She had had an accident at work and broken her foot and had got hooked on the opiates she took to take away the pain. I didn't know that she kept taking them after her foot had healed.

The kids began telling me stories of how she would take them out on Saturday mornings, supposedly to go shopping, and she would stop at one doctor's clinic after another and pick up drugs. Then she would drive while she was high. When I learned about her behavior, I tried to take some of the drugs, just a small amount so she wouldn't notice, and hide them. However, rather than throwing them away, I started taking them as well. I realized I would soon be getting strung out on them, and I couldn't afford to do that.

I was so miserable at this time that I would cry out to God in the shower, asking Him to deliver me from this whole situation. I should have been more specific and asked him not to include a prison term in His salvation from the problem!! Be careful what you ask for as you just may get it!

One night my wife wanted to go out and get more pills at the hospital, but she was already too high to drive, especially since she was going to take the kids with her. I grabbed the keys from her, and while she was fighting me like a wildcat, I pushed her away. She stumbled and fell and banged her head. I finally dragged her onto the bed and held her down while I called her grandfather to come and pick the kids up. I waited until I knew they were nearly there, and then I jumped up, got my briefcase and go bag (which I had Elijah bring), got in the car, and split. I saw the grandparents at the corner as I was leaving the property. My little son, Elijah, was running after me, in his boxers, with *his* little get away bag, wanting to come with me.

She had already called the police. Her grandfather told the police that I had called them and they were there to get the kids as she was too high to look after them. The police told him that she had said I had pistol whipped her. They gave her a field sobriety test, and by this time she was able to pass it.

I called Garland, her grandfather, to see what was going on, and he told me what the police had told him. I then checked every day to see if a warrant had showed up in the computer. Eventually there was one, but it took a few months. Meanwhile, she had talked me into coming back home.

During that time, Hannah went to her school counselor, complaining about what was going on in the house. Both kids would complain to me about their mother, and I would tell them what I was trying to do. I told her to talk to the school counselor, who I thought would send someone to help. Instead, CPS came and took the children and put them into foster care. I had to petition to get the children sent over to the grandparents. Their mother was against it, but the court agreed with me, saying that it was better for them to be with natural family.

During this time, Donna had talked to her lawyer, and they had worked out that they could claim domestic violence on me. To strengthen her case, she went to stay at a battered woman's shelter which she ultimately was kicked out of for using. During the court case, however, she had a change of heart after going into a drug rehab and testified to the judge that she had never told the police I had pistol whipped her and that, in fact, I was trying to save her life that night. But the police had her on tape, saying what she said, so her lawyer convinced her that she would go to prison for lying if she didn't stop arguing with the D.A. (In many cases, battered wives do change their testimony, so the police still thought I had been abusing her).

Once again, I was given the option of 25 to life if I didn't take a deal. My lawyer advised me to take the deal, as it is very difficult to prove innocence in a domestic violence case. The three strike law was still in existence at that time, and I couldn't play Russian roulette with my life, so I took the deal of four years with 80 percent to serve.

I was so angry with God at this time. Once again, I felt I was innocent of all charges, and I had already taken a deal when I was accused of kidnapping Billy and Sarah. Now, here I was again, having done nothing wrong, having to serve a prison sentence.

Just as the apostle Paul told the Galatians, "We reap what we sow."

I was sent to a reception center in Los Angeles. I expected to be sent to one of two prisons near where I lived so the family could visit me. A few months after being there, I was called down to the office and told to pack my things, as I was going to San Quentin up in San Francisco, which everyone knows is a maximum security prison and has a death row and every kind of hardened prisoner. I was very apprehensive and could not believe where my life was heading after I had been clean for years and serving God with my life. I also knew I wasn't going to be getting any visits from my family.

I later found out that the whites and the skinheads at the LA prison had a riot the next day. God had, once again, saved me from that. All the way in the prison bus, I was thinking what had I done wrong to deserve this kind of cruel and unusual punishment. However, I was not yet ready to give up, as I knew God always had something up his sleeve, like He was having the last laugh on me.

During my time at the reception center, I was lucky to get a Bible to read. As soon as I arrived at the prison and found out there was a chapel, I went there forthwith. I saw a brochure in the chapel; it said that the local Baptist seminary was sponsoring a program within the prison called CLD. I immediately signed up, but the devil immediately tried to make me unable to go to school. I got a job that conflicted with the classes. Then they tried to transfer me out of San Quentin because of my bad back. There was, however, always a guard or counselor to help me see my goal through.

One of my classmates in the CLD program was one of the original co-founders of the Crips gang. He was now a believer and active in chapel activities. He ran the program office and was able to get me a job in the office where the Captain, Associate Wardens, and all the brass worked. I was responsible for doing all the clerical work and was able to get away at night to go to seminary classes and to use the computer in the office for my homework.

One of my classes was a practicum for evangelism, so I set up a grilled cheese stand in the prison. I got a heating element from a hot water pot and used the bottom of a large can as my grill. I would buy blocks of cheese and loaves of bread from the kitchen workers. My stand was known to serve any race or religion. I used it as a means to share religious tracts, and I got to talk to many inmates about my testimony.

California Years

Now I could see what God had in mind. I had tried to go to Bible College many times, but with a family, I could not afford the time or money. Here I was being offered a free education (along with free text books) through the seminary, along with free housing and food. God works in mysterious ways, but I wish it wasn't always prison for me!!

I was wondering why I hadn't heard anything from Donna. I had showed her how to fill out the paperwork to get me exonerated. I didn't expect not to hear from her, and I thought I would only be in prison a short time until she could get it sorted out. One day when I was able to get hold of a cell phone, I called my daughter Hannah and she told me that her mother had married another drug addict and had already had and lost one baby and was currently pregnant with another. She hadn't seen or heard from her in a while and was still living with the great-grandparents.

I was in total shock. I thought I would get out and get back to my family, and now it was all in shreds. I had left Donna with the keys to everything, and now I found out that all my stuff had been sold to support her drug habit. I had nothing in the world. She didn't even keep the photographs of my other children.

I was able to graduate from both diploma programs the seminary offered while I was in prison. During that time, I regularly wrote letters to the director of facilities for the Golden Gate campus, applying for work as a maintenance man, naming my teachers as references. Finally, after numerous letters, the facilities director started asking these people if they knew me and what they thought of me. He told me to see him when I got out and he might have a job for me. All of us in the CLD program were told that we could apply to have the credits from the classes we had taken in prison used in the regular seminary program. If I took the required classes and maintained a good grade point (A-), I could receive a master's degree through the Master's by Exception program. This excited me, as I never thought I would ever get the chance to get my Master's degree.

CHAPTER SEVEN

After Prison

As I was preparing to get out of San Quentin, everything that could go wrong, did go wrong. I was trying to transfer my parole from Riverside County to the county where the seminary was located. When I was released, I had to get on a bus and report within 24 hours to Riverside County probation department and request a transfer back to San Francisco. When I got there, the transfer had already been approved, so I immediately got back on a bus and headed back up to San Francisco. It seemed like I had three days with no sleep, but I showed up at the office of the facility director at Golden Gate Seminary to apply for a maintenance job.

After an interview, I was given a job working maintenance, a place to stay, and, as a seminary employee, free education to do my Master's degree. I had stayed at a local shelter while my apartment was being painted. Now I was like a pig in mud – working during the day doing maintenance, living in my own apartment, and going to school at night.

The seminary classes were very difficult for me, who had not been a student for so long, and I had to maintain a 3.2 grade point average to be considered for the master's by exception. I was able to use some credits for what I had already done, and a lot of the classes were similar to those I had taken in prison, using the same textbooks, so that gave me some advantage. I also got a lot of help from one of the teachers, Reta Beall, who edited my papers (and this book) and taught me about academic writing. She also had to explain to me why plagiarism was wrong!!

After a very busy year at the seminary and no contact with my family, I became quite lonely. I had originally planned to try reuniting with my kids once I got out of prison, but those hopes were dashed when the grandparents told me I could talk to them by phone but could not visit them for at least a year. I later learned that they would harass my children when I would call them and take away some of their privileges, like their phones or Internet. They were engaging in parental alienation, and this was all so difficult for me. I had only two options – to go on a violent spree of vengeance or give it totally to God to work out. Fortunately, I took the latter option.

My bachelor pad at the seminary was not being used like I thought it would. Any woman I asked out from the seminary seemed to feel threatened by me. Nevertheless, I had a feeling that God had a special wife for me, but I felt like I didn't deserve one. I talked to one of my teachers, Don Beall, and he said, "Whoever deserves anything that we get?" However, other people asked me to think realistically. If I wanted a good woman, why would she ever want me, once she knew about my record. I could only agree with that thought, but somehow deep down I still had hope that God could do the impossible.

I decided to help God out by trying online dating. I thought I heard God say "China," so I decided to begin looking for a Chinese girl. Actually, I wasn't sure whether it was God speaking or my stomach, as I love Chinese food. Pretty soon, I was getting all sorts of responses from women from the Philippines, Africa, and other places in Asia. I soon realized they were all after an American passport. I switched back to America only, but one last Asian profile somehow slipped past the filters. I noticed that someone had looked at my profile. I was expecting a 22-year-old Asian girl. She was not, however, Chinese, as I had expected, but a white Australian woman who was working as a teacher in Hong Kong. I also noticed, looking at her profile, that she was quite clear about what she would and would not accept. She had set up some hoops that I needed to jump through just to contact her. I liked her style and thought I could copy her requirements, but seeing I had just been lectured about plagiarism from Reta, I thought I should ask her first.

When I first contacted Jill, she asked me to send more pictures, as she couldn't tell what I looked like from my profile picture, which was taken at my graduation from the CLD program in prison. I thought she was quite bossy, but something kept me going back. Soon, we were chatting on Skype. Once we had done that, she told me we could go back to emailing now that she knew I was really an American.

She was thinking of going to Bethel church in Redding, California, for a seminar over the summer break, and I encouraged her to come and see me if she did. I said I would drive her up to Redding if she would come. She visited me in July for one week, and we did go up to Redding for the weekend. All during that week my stomach was in knots, and I couldn't eat. I didn't know whether it was demonic oppression or just that I liked her so much that it was making me nervous.

At the end of that week, I took her to the airport to fly out, and I couldn't believe how sad I was feeling as I had to let her go. We had talked about a relationship, but it seemed like having a long distance one was too difficult. She was having an operation for a lump on her ear soon after she got back to Hong Kong, and I told her I wanted to be with her during that week. I wasn't working due to a back injury, so I had the time.

As I was driving back from the airport, I felt like God was telling me to go visit a jewelry shop that I knew of and buy her a ring. I didn't have much money at that time, but I knew better than to disobey God. When I got to the store, I told the salesman that I was buying a ring for a classy lady but I didn't have much money, so what could he do for me. He told me he had the exact ring for me, and he went into the back room to get it. When I saw that it had a pink diamond in the middle, I knew it was the right one, as she loved everything pink and she had seen some halo designs that she said she liked.

I flew to Hong Kong two weeks later, supposedly for a week or two, but before I left, I was impressed to get rid of all my belongings and take what I needed with me, as I might not be coming back, so that is what I did. I packed up my apartment, gave lots of stuff away, and took all that I needed with me.

Once I was in Hong Kong, Jill and I began spending more time together; we both knew that we were meant for each other. I suggested that I finish up my Master's degree online and stay in Hong Kong so we could pursue a relationship. She agreed, so that is what we did. She had a penthouse flat upstairs I could use, so I was all set.

It was a big learning curve for me to be exposed to all her friends and family, and I often felt out of my comfort zone. She took me to Australia to meet her family at Christmas time. I really liked them and envied her having a real family who enjoyed spending time together. I liked all her friends also, but it was overwhelming to be introduced to so many. I had spent my life mostly in isolation because when a person lives a life of crime, he does not want people knowing anything about his business. Jill seemed to share openly with everyone about what was happening in her life, and this was very strange to me.

She had told me that her parent's wedding anniversary was on October 10, so I proposed to her on that night. She said yes, so we were officially engaged. We got married on March 28 of the following year at a beach on the Gold Coast, in Australia. My life had really expanded to traveling all over the world.

Living in Hong Kong was a very different experience. It was so hot and humid most of the time. Jill had told me that everything was air conditioned in Hong Kong, but what she omitted to tell me was that I would be drenched with sweat just walking to the air-conditioned bus or train. I really didn't like always feeling hot.

Jill and I had many discussions about our future. She always encouraged me to try to get my kids back, but we didn't know how that would come about because the great-grandparents (who were my ex's grandparents) were so hostile to me. We prayed about it every night. Sometimes my daughter Hannah would call me when she was away from the house, but then her grandparents would check her phone records and punish her for calling me, so she had her boyfriend keep in touch with us and let us know what was happening with her. Then Hannah contacted us one day to say her grandmother had hit her across the face and pulled her hair and the police had been called, so she had been put into foster care. This now meant I had total access to Hannah and I could call her any time.

We made a plan to go and visit that summer (2015) and appear in court with Hannah. We had to talk with CPS first, and they had to be at all our meetings with Hannah. We were not sure if we would even be able to see my son Elijah, who had been told lots of lies about me. The grandparents used to scare the kids by saying I would come and kidnap them, and they would buy pepper spray for them to use to protect themselves. I had been very apprehensive about even going to Oklahoma, where they lived, as I was afraid they might call the police on some trumped up charge and get me arrested.

However, God had really gone before us and prepared the way. The grandparents couldn't have been nicer to us, and the grandmother even apologized about how she had treated me. She acknowledged that I had changed a lot over the years, and they really liked Jill. My son was a bit cool with us on the first meeting, as he didn't know what to expect, but he warmed up over the week we were there.

In the middle of the night during that week, both Jill and I couldn't sleep. We had been considering three options for ministry: going to Thailand where we had a house and doing ministry with children, going back to Australia where Jill was from and where we had property on the beach, or building something on land I had in Houston and doing a homeless ministry there. Jill and I had shared our options with her friends, and they were also praying about what we should do. One of Jill's good friends, an older man, called us after we had visited them at Christmas time. He told Jill he felt he had a word from God for us, and she asked him to write it down in an email. Basically, he said that we should stay on in HK and finish her contract and that he felt like God was leading us somewhere that we hadn't considered yet. He believed God was going to do a new thing with us.

We were seriously praying about all these three options and had asked God to show us over that summer holiday what He wanted us to do, but in the middle of the night, I just knew we should be moving to Oklahoma to be with my kids. What was the point of saving the world if I couldn't save my own kids? I knew I had a responsibility to them. God had so clearly gone before us and greased the skids, so it was like "jump on the board and ride the wave rather than paddle out and look for a wave." Jill was awake also, so I shared my thoughts with her, and she immediately felt it was the right thing to do. We now had a concrete direction for our future, a sense of true north, and we knew we were in the middle of God's plan for us.

Jill, as a teacher, had holidays in October for one week, so we planned to go back and see the kids again in Oklahoma and look for a house to buy. During our earlier visit, the judge had asked that we come back to attend Hannah's court case, and they accommodated us by hearing it that week. We looked at what seemed like 50 houses. We found the house we wanted, one with five bedrooms, and on the day we were to leave, we learned that our offer had been accepted. We also found another house, one to be used as a rental, and we bought it the same week. We paid less for two houses than we had expected to pay for one house.

We went back to Oklahoma several times to attend court with Hannah, and now that CPS knew we were moving to Oklahoma, they wanted to place her with me. However, we knew that by the time we got there, she would only have one month before she turned 18. We knew her plan was to get her own apartment or move in with her boyfriend, which we had all advised her against. However, she needed to make her own mistakes. I knew by experience that it wouldn't last long, and I determined that we would be there to pick up the pieces.

Prior to all of these things happening, I had managed to finish my Master's degree online in May of 2015, and I tried to get a job in Hong Kong, but my age and inability to speak Chinese were against me. I was bored at home all day, so I started fiddling around on the Internet, and I watched some posts on how to sell things online. I watched many online webinars and did lots of research and started selling online in a very small way that December. From our very first month of selling online on Amazon, we made a small amount of money, and each month we doubled the sales of the month before. We were lucky to be living in Hong Kong, as we could go and visit the factories in China from which most Americans who sell on Amazon buy their products. We are still involved in this business. It has been challenging to try and anticipate what is popular in the market, but God seems to help us all the time to pick products that are good sellers.

We brought my son to Hong Kong the following summer. He turned 14 while he was with us, and we gave him lots of gifts for his birthday. When Jill got off school at the end of June, we took him to Australia with us for two weeks. He got to visit the beach in Queensland for a week, and then we drove to Sydney and had "Christmas in July" with her family in the Hunter Valley, where her niece owns a resort. Australia is hot in December, so they like to experience Christmas in the cold sometimes, and many restaurants and resorts offer a Christmas in July package, complete with Christmas carols, trees, and gifts.

After that, we took him to Thailand, where we own a house, and had a week there with lots of fun riding motorbikes before going back to Hong Kong and China. When he got home, he was the envy of all his friends. He had previously been the poor kid who had to live with his great-grandparents because his mom was a drug addict and his dad was in prison. Now he was an international playboy. We bonded a lot over this summer as father and son. I am still amazed at how God can change our circumstances in just a short time.

It was now time to prepare to make the move to Oklahoma. I got our house in Hong Kong painted and ready, and the movers came to pack up all our stuff for the move. All of this was a huge undertaking; Jill had spent 23 years of her life in Hong Kong, and she had to decide what to keep and what to sell and what to give away. She wanted to take her dogs with her, which I thought was crazy, but she insisted they were part of the family and they were coming with us. That meant we had to buy crates for them and take them to the airport with us, along with four huge suitcases and two large carry-on bags as well as computer bags and handbags and my CPAP bag. When we arrived in Los Angeles, we needed our own van to transport everything to the hotel. The dogs were amazing although they must have been very scared with all that was happening.

We flew from L.A. to Dallas the following day, as we needed a big enough aircraft to take the large dog crate. We then rented a U-Haul to take all our belongings and the two dogs to Oklahoma City. We looked like a circus, hauling all those bags and two dogs at the airport.

We arrived safely in Oklahoma on August 21, 2016, and got a hotel for the first week while we renovated and painted one of our rental houses. We moved in after the first week and painted and did up the house while we were living there. After six weeks, we found out the tenants in our big house were moving out, so we moved into our big house and rented out the smaller house.

Hannah broke up with her boyfriend after just a few months and asked if could she move in with us. We hoped that she had learned her lesson. She came and lived with us for a year, and I hope I was able to be a father to her during this time. We didn't always agree on things, and she could be difficult to live with at times.

At first, my son was still living with his grandparents and spending weekends with us, but he was soon spending half the week at our place. We made an agreement with him that he would stay part time with the great-grandparents until his 82-year-old grandfather passed away. He had been at death's door on many occasions. We felt bad for him that he was living with old people and was working like an orderly for them.

His great-grandfather passed away in August of 2017, while we were on a road trip to visit Jill's aunt in Utah. Elijah immediately moved in with us full time and hasn't gone back to the grandparents' home, except to visit a few times. Our bond has grown stronger and stronger.

Jill and I took one month over Christmas 2017 to visit her family and our house in Thailand. Unfortunately, I slipped on the tiles at her brother's house in Sydney and fell, landing hard on my hip on the bottom step of the staircase. I was taken by ambulance to the hospital because I was in such incredible pain and couldn't stand on my leg. They thought I had broken my hip. I also had a slight heart attack from the intense pain I was in. I spent three nights and four days in the hospital over Christmas. The only silver lining was that I didn't have to socialize with all the family and friends over this period. We were told that the hospital bill was over $2400 per day, so I tried to get out of hospital as quickly as possible. I ended up with a huge hematoma on my right leg that reached from my knee up along my entire hamstring and thigh.

I tried to rest up at the house, and we were due to leave on December 31 to fly to Thailand. I felt very unwell but wanted to keep going with our journey, so we flew overnight to Malaysia, had a two-hour wait in the airport, and then flew on to Bangkok where a taxi was waiting to drive us several hours south to our house. I could barely breath and was feeling worse and worse. Jill wanted to take me to the emergency room, but I was stubborn and didn't want to go. I asked her to contact my doctor in the US and explain my symptoms, and after 36 hours he told her to take me to hospital immediately as I probably had a lung embolism. Sure enough, lung scans revealed that I had several lung clots and a DVT in my right leg. No wonder I had been feeling so bad.

The doctors said it was a miracle that I had survived the trip at all as the lung clots had passed through my heart already. That process usually kills a person, but they were small enough to pass through the arteries. I stayed in hospital for 10 days, and I was soon walking around and feeling better as they were giving me blood thinners and lots of morphine. I got out on Jan. 11, and we went out for lunch and for a massage. That was a huge mistake. I began feeling bad again that evening and thought maybe I should go back to the hospital, but I had an appointment on the 13th anyway, so I waited until then. My doctor immediately readmitted me, as she knew that blood was going back into the hematoma from the blood thinners, and now the hematoma had gone from 14cm to 49 cm, around 19 inches, in length. The doctors were very concerned.

We were in a smaller hospital in a little town called Hua Hin in Thailand, and I was concerned about the knowledge of doctors in a third world country. The care was excellent, though, and for a lot of the time I had my own private suite, which was even nicer than hospital rooms in America. However, they felt they couldn't contain the bleeding, and one of the doctors had tried to aspirate blood from the hematoma but was not successful. After a few days, they felt they needed to move me to their headquarters in Bangkok, the main city in Thailand. After two weeks in the Bangkok hospital, the hematoma had stopped bleeding and the lung clots had gone down to 10 percent of their size, so we felt we were safe to fly back to the US. Once again, God had saved my life, but I don't know why I go through these kinds of things on a regular basis. I felt like something good should come out of this time, so Jill and I began spending our days trying to set up our houses for ministry and writing this book to encourage others, like me, that there is always hope for a better future.

Since moving to Oklahoma, we have gotten involved in several ministries. We have started teaching at the men's prison in Lexington with Prison Fellowship. We have done two different classes so far, each lasting around 12 weeks, and the guys are very receptive to us.

We had been attending a local church, where we heard about some houses for women which they support. Since that is what I did before, we were interested in doing some ministry with the homeless or those who had come out of prison with the large house. It is tailor made for running a group home. I feel that I have a lot to give with all that I have learned in my life, and I want to be a beacon of hope, sharing with others that no matter how poor their circumstances and how badly life has treated them, God has a good plan for them and He is able to bring beauty out of ashes.

Now we are using our real estate in Oklahoma City to provide houses for women who have recently come out of prison or for drug addicts who want to live in a sober living environment. We hope to be able to help those who need help and to give back because of how God has blessed our lives.

As of the time of writing, we have now given over two of our homes to our church ministry and once again, we have seen the church work together to create something awesome. Our small rental (which we have named Jenny's house in honor of my daughter) really needed some work, and volunteers from the church painted the whole house, put down new turf, created a garden, and turned the garage into a new bedroom for the house manager, including installing a shower and toilet. Volunteers have also bought a new refrigerator and oven for the house and cleaned the carpets. We have been overwhelmed with how much work has been done to support women in transition.

We have also moved out of our big house and made it available to our church. Seven women are currently living there, along with a house supervisor. Volunteers even helped us pack up and move to a house we rented in a gated community north of the city where the academics and environment for my son are superior.

God has blessed us abundantly as we have sought to follow Him and make ourselves available for ministry. We have been able to get our son into a good school that will challenge him academically, and he is already exceling.

Update on My Children

At the time of writing, my oldest daughter, Christeena, has been in and out of jail for drugs. She has lost custody of her children. I am not sure what percentage can be attributed to my past life, and it makes me feel very guilty, as her life has not turned out any better than mine was in my early years. She is, however, a believer and was well trained as a child. She seeks out the chapel or Christian community when she ends up in jail. We still keep in touch when she is out of jail, and we hope that she will be able to break the cycle at some time.

As previously mentioned, my second daughter, Jenny, died of a drug overdose at the very young age of 21. We know that she loved Jesus, so I look forward to the day when I will see her again in heaven. We have dedicated one of our transitional houses in her name, hoping that no other parent needs to get the devastating news that their daughter has died.

My oldest son, William Dew, is schizophrenic and is living with his mother. He spent some time with us in Oklahoma in early 2017, and I learned a new appreciation for his mother, who is willing to take care of him and all the medical appointments etc. that are required to help him stay on track. We stay in touch by phone.

My third daughter, Sarah, is in Arizona and is fighting for custody of her own daughter. How history repeats itself. She is a real go getter and works hard to support herself. She is very creative and has opened her own shop to sell antiques and other crafts as well as work a full-time job.

The youngest two are both here with me in Oklahoma. Hannah is attending college and working full time and has recently been made an assistant manager of a 7-11 store. She has huge potential in life and I hope she can realize it.

My youngest son, Elijah, lives with us and is doing very well at school, where he is a junior. He is currently in all AP classes and doing football, as well as working part time at McDonalds, so I hope he can handle all that is on his plate and still do well academically.

Final Thoughts

The telling of this story began as I lay in a hospital bed. I had time to process how God was working in my life as I remembered the past and celebrated the present. I related it to Jill, who recorded what I said and retold it in her own words. At this point, I want to use my own words to share some final comments.

There is only one reason I am undergoing the embarrassment of this book and that may be for you. This is a story of grace mostly, but not without love. Over the years, God has been with me in all the filthy places I have taken Him, and He has protected me every time without exception. I, of course, should have been dead many times through the years, but He has relentlessly and overwhelmingly come to the rescue every time. A very important part in all this that must not be forgotten is that I feel clean! I do not deserve any forgiveness from God, yet He has completely forgiven me, and I actually feel it. I am working on forgiving myself mostly nowadays and there is always another area of weakness revealing itself. I continue to ask Him to examine my heart.

If you are like me and have struggled or are struggling with your faith, my best advice is wait.

Isaiah 40:31-1 – "But they that wait upon the Lord shall renew their strength; they shall mount up with wings as eagles; they shall run, and not be weary; and they shall walk, and not faint."

We are saved because of Him and nothing we do, so know that his grace is sufficient.

We will prevail and He can change us from within in a way totally impossible without him.

There is nothing you can do to deserve His grace, but if you are disregarding his commands without remorse or any desire to change, that is not what grace means. I suggest you reexamine your salvation.

I think one of the hardest things to do is break through the denial and layers of rationalization and justification. We, however, need to take that to the Lord and ask Him, as David did, to examine our hearts and reveal in us those things we do that are not pleasing to Him.

When I was first in recovery and had to look for character defects, I did not see any!! I cheated and called my ex-wife because she had a list I had tuned out for years. If you can't see your own defects, ask those closest to you; they will tell you.

Sometimes I feel like a soldier who has left his platoon behind. However, I have gone into institutional places and ministered. Words can't begin to describe the feeling of joy I get out of just being an encouragement to those in jail or institutions of any kind.

If you are incarcerated or in any place with a chaplain, please contact them for free copies of this book.

We continue to seek opportunities for ministry and are seeing God bless our business, which keeps us very busy. I am recovering from my sickness early this year and have just been given a clean bill of health from the doctors.

I trust this book will bless you and give you hope that there is always a hope and a future for each one of us.

Jeremiah 29:11 – "I know the thoughts I have for you, says the Lord, plans to give you a hope and a future".

Made in the USA
Columbia, SC
24 July 2022